MW01254771

The Human Body Detectives in a must-have in every child
teach how the human body functions in a fun & engaging
fuel their bodies in a healthy way. These books are a wor
and future scientists.
Antoinette de Janasz
President, The Twooth Timer Company

The Human Body Detective Series is a must for all parents. If you're trying to get your kids to eat
right, stay healthy or exercise then these books are for you. They're destined to become a classic.
Sharon Silver
Proactive Parenting

I love that the stories weave food and nutrition into the narrative to give kids an understanding
of why eating whole foods is so important. If you're looking for something that educates and
entertains children – while teaching parents as well – don't miss out on this modern "physiological"
version of the Magic School Bus series.
Mel Hicks
President, Big Time Tea Company

My children and I love the Human Body Detective Series! I have never seen a children's story
book packed with this much interesting educational information. In addition to being great
adventure stories, they teach the child so much about how the body works. In addition to the facts
embedded in the story, there is a ton of additional information at the back of the book including
a glossary. I have a Ph.D. in biochemistry and I've learned a thing or two from these books! My 3
year old loves to listen to the exciting stories even though he doesn't understand it all. My 6 year
old loves to read the stories and understands them. My 9 year old reads the stories and studies
the information at the back of the book. Kids who read these books will be way ahead of the
curve by the time they get to health class in middle school.
Annie Pryor, Ph.D
www.stopthestomachflu.com

Heather Manley, N.D.
www.drheathernd.com

Copyright © 2014 by Heather Manley, N.D.
All rights reserved. Printed and published in the United States of America.

No part of this book may be used or reproduced
in any form without written permission from the author.

For reproduction of any part of this book
or for more information please contact:
Heather Manley, N.D.
email: drheather@drheathernd.com
www.drheathernd.com | www.humanbodydetectives.com

human body detectives®

Brainiacs

CASE FILE #5

Dr. Heather Manley

It was Tuesday morning after a three-day weekend; Merrin and Pearl were moving s l o w l y as they prepared for school. They had spent the weekend with their Uncle Nick who was a brain scientist, and Pearl had been mesmerized by some of their talks.

As they lazily ate their eggs and drank their blueberry smoothies, Pearl couldn't help herself from pulling out her computer and researching information about the brain.

"Wow, Merrin, did you know that your brain is 80% water?" Pearl said in amazement.

"No, I didn't," Merrin said over her shoulder as she walked out of the kitchen toward her room to get ready for school.

"And guess what? The human brain weighs about three pounds and an elephant has the biggest brain. So fascinating!" Pearl added as she put her computer to the side and got up from her breakfast stool. She needed to get moving or she was going to be late.

Herbal Tea Bags

2

Merrin was clueless as to what Pearl was jibber-jabbing about. Even though it made no sense to her, she knew it made perfect sense to Pearl. There was no denying that Pearl had a curious and creative mind. *I have an inkling she's up to something*, Merrin thought.

Merrin was right. Pearl was on a mission. Her uncle had piqued her curiosity about the brain. She wondered how exactly it worked and how it got the rest of the body to do things.

After the girls finished getting ready for school, they both headed back to the kitchen to pack their lunches.

"I'm going to add some walnuts and **broccoli** to my lunch; Uncle Nick said they are great brain foods," Pearl told Merrin.

"Why are you so interested in the brain?" Merrin asked quizzically.

"Well, **the brain is super cool**. It's like a living computer communicating all day long, right inside your body! Don't you remember what Uncle Nick said? The brain gathers information and then gives the body instructions on how to act and react. If you didn't have a brain, Merrin, you wouldn't be able to feel something hot, run away from something scary, or learn French. Your brain runs EVERYTHING!"

Merrin shrugged and then said, "Well, he did say some pretty cool things, like that your brain can generate enough **electricity** to power a light bulb! That's pretty incredible."

"Yes, crazy amazing," Pearl remarked.

"Oops, I forgot my math homework," Merrin said, heading back to her room. "Pearl, grab your backpack," Merrin added. "We need to get going to school."

Ignoring her, Pearl picked up her computer again and began reading. "The nervous system is made up of the nerves, spinal cord, and the brain."

Pearl thought about how lucky she and Merrin were to be Human Body Detectives with the ability to go into people's bodies and see how they work. And then she remembered a Human Body Detectives adventure where they got to see and learn about the bones in the body. They had also learned that the spinal cord runs along your back with the vertebrae protecting it and all its nerves.

Pearl continued reading. "The biggest part of the brain, the cerebrum, is divided into two equal parts called hemispheres. The right hemisphere controls movements on the left side of the body, and the left hemisphere controls movements on the right side of the body." *That's interesting*, thought Pearl.

"Scientists believe that the right hemisphere also helps you think about abstract things like music, colors, and shapes. They say that the left hemisphere helps with things like math, logic, and speech."

Pearl understood that the cerebrum not only has two hemispheres, but it also has four distinct areas, called lobes, which have their own jobs: occipital lobe for vision; the temporal lobe for smell and sound; the frontal lobe for conscious thought, memory, and personality; and the parietal lobe for integrating information.

I need to get inside a brain and see for myself how it works.

Then an idea came to her. Pearl loudly announced, "We need to get into my teacher, Ms. Anderson's, brain. She is SO smart and seeing her brain in action would be perfect."

Pearl raced to Merrin's room to tell her the plan, but didn't find her. She was excited and wondered which side and part of her brain she was using to have these feelings. "Wow, the human body is so complex and interesting!" she muttered to herself.

Finally she heard Merrin, basically screaming, from the kitchen, "Get a move on it, Pearl! I don't want to be late!"

Right, I don't want to be late for school either. Pearl grabbed her backpack and headed out the front door, all the while contemplating her plan—her plan to get into Ms. Anderson's brain with Merrin.

As they were heading to school, Pearl begged Merrin to walk her all the way to her classroom, before going on to her seventh grade room. It wasn't too hard to convince her because Merrin adored Ms. Anderson and was more than happy to say hello to her. But Merrin had no idea what Pearl was really up to.

When they arrived, Pearl snuggled up to Merrin while she was visiting with Ms. Anderson. Merrin tried to brush her off, but as she did, she gently nudged Ms. Anderson's elbow, which resulted in the tea mug that Ms. Anderson was holding to jostle a bit. It looked like it might spill. Pearl realized this was the moment; she knew they would be missed for only a second or two—in real time—and she wanted to get inside a brain and a **SUPER** intelligent one! What if they could watch how Ms. Anderson's brain reacted to the hot tea that might spill on her?

As the tea was getting ready to spill, Pearl gently closed her eyes, nestled closer to Merrin, and began visualizing them inside Ms. Anderson's brain. The familiar dizziness and the twirling and twisting sensation they always felt when they were about to go on a Human Body Detective adventure settled in... But it didn't last long. Pearl heard Merrin sigh and mutter, "Pearl, what are you doing?"

When the dizzy feeling stopped, Pearl looked down and saw that they were standing on something white and hard.

She immediately knew they were on a bone, but she had no idea which one—there are 206 in the human body, after all. Plus, why would they be on a bone? They were trying to get to the brain.

"Are we on bone?" Merrin asked.

"Yes, we have to be. Yet I have no idea why. The plan was to get to Ms. Anderson's brain to see how it works. This is all so strange."

"Oh gosh, Pearl. Where have you taken us? And what is that rubbery looking thing next to us?" Merrin questioned.

Merrin looked confused. But then she heard a SHRIEK that sounded far away.

"Ouch," they heard Ms. Anderson cry, grasping her leg. "That tea is hot!"

"Oh no," Pearl said."Ms. Anderson must have spilled hot tea on herself."

Pearl thought for a moment and observed her surroundings. The bone was big. Perhaps the biggest bone in the body and that elastic band—
"That's it!" Pearl exclaimed. "We're on the femur, the biggest bone in the body. And that **rubbery** thing is the sciatic nerve, the longest and widest nerve in the body."

Suddenly they saw a rush of flashing bright lights coming their way. It looked like hundreds of moving stars in the sky.

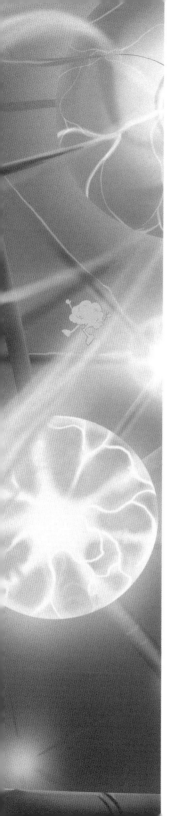

They were moving *fast*—really *fast*. Pearl knew they had to get out of their way; they couldn't risk getting knocked over and plunging somewhere else in the body or, worse, losing each other.

Pearl began to worry a bit.

"What is up with all these lights?" Merrin questioned.

"They're nerve impulses! I remember Uncle Nick talking about them. Something is happening to Ms. Anderson. The sciatic nerve has been stimulated; it must have been when the hot tea spilled on her. These nerve impulses need to send a message to the brain so it can tell the body how to react. Hopefully Ms. Anderson's nerve impulse will travel really *fast* so she pulls her leg away and more tea doesn't spill on her, causing her burn to blister!"

"Ok, Smarty, what's a neuron?"

Pearl smiled and answered, "A neuron is a bundle of nerves that receives messages in the body and helps deliver them to the brain. When the brain gets the message it will make actions happen."

"What's going to happen?"

"Spilling the hot tea on her leg alerted the sciatic nerve... That's why we're here on the femur. Wow! This is going to be great! Now a nerve impulse will travel by the sciatic nerve to the spinal cord to get to the brain, and then the nerve impulse will go back to her leg so she will move it out of the way."

"Impressive, but a tad confusing," Merrin said with a look of interest on her face.

Relieved that Merrin was not frightened and even seemed excited, Pearl decided to throw in some of the trivia she had just read before school that morning. "Wait 'til you hear this. An entire nerve impulse passes through a neuron in about seven milliseconds—faster than a lightning strike!"

And then Merrin surprised Pearl.

"Pearl, let's follow one. Maybe it will help us learn what's happening to Ms. Anderson. Jump on the next nerve impulse that comes our way!" Pearl was a little unsure about this idea. There were hundreds headed toward them. If they did jump on one, it would take them to the spinal cord and brain, which would be a really cool adventure. Before she could think more about it, Merrin grabbed onto Pearl's hand and quickly inched her way toward an impulse that was passing by. As Merrin and Pearl crouched down and got ready to jump, they felt a light breeze brush against their cheeks. As they leaned in more, the majestic yet swift impulse picked them up and off they went.

They sped rapidly on their very energetic and determined nerve impulse. Both girls huddled together, their hair blowing back, and they both wore wide smiles on their faces. This was better than any roller coaster ride.

Merrin pointed and said loudly, "Hey, Pearl, those look like the vertebrae. I remember what they look like from our travels in the skeletal system."

Merrin was right. Once inside the spine they would enter the central nervous system, which consists of the spinal cord and brain. They were on the highway to the brain.

Both sisters *yelped* with excitement as they accelerated and made a sharp turn into the dark tunnel of the spinal cord. Immediately, they found themselves among lots of strange branch- or finger-like things.

"Dendrites," Pearl exclaimed.

"Huh?" Merrin looked at her sister.

"They are part of the neuron. Remember, neurons are found mostly in the spinal cord and brain. They help the nerve impulses travel longer distances, like all the way up the spinal cord."

As they moved through the dendrite branches, still on their nerve impulse, they landed on something white and began bouncing from one white thing to the next—like jumping from one mini trampoline to another.

"What are these things we're being bounced on?"
Merrin asked in a shaky, muffled voice. It was hard to talk when bopping up and down.

"These are the nodes of Ranvier. They are on the axon, which helps the impulse move at a tremendous speed and get the message to the brain. With the help of over 100 billion neurons in the brain, the body and brain are constantly communicating by passing the nerve impulse from neuron to neuron."

Pearl was correct, and she suddenly realized that the real Human Body Detectives adventure was now in full speed.

Merrin looked around in amazement and remembered the time she spilled hot soup on her leg. It was painful! She felt bad for Ms. Anderson.

"Merrin, hold on! I think we're coming to the end of this neuron!"

That was the last thing Merrin heard. Their hands slipped apart. Pearl went to the left of the dendrite and Merrin, to the right. Although she was still moving *fast*, Merrin suddenly saw what looked like a junction of some sort looming ahead of her. She couldn't see anything on the other side, but there had to be another neuron, right?

Oh, no. I'm going to fall off this dendrite. She started to scream. "**Pearl, where are you?**" she yelled.

It was no use. She was alone and had to think—and recall. "Wait," she muttered. "The frontal lobe of my brain stores all my memory." She thought of this because she used to beg it to remember all the math equations she had to memorize. Focusing on her frontal lobe, she thought hard.

Calmly, Merrin took a deep breath and said to herself, "I'm at the end of the axon, part of the neuron, and I need to get to the next dendrite via a synapse.

"That's it! The junction! It's a synapse between each neuron like a bridge for the information to travel over. Once the impulse I'm on travels down the axon to the end, called the axon terminal, it will hop over a synapse to the next dendrite. Maybe on the other side of the synapse, I'll meet up with Pearl again!"

Merrin grew more confident, and as she approached the synapse she braced herself to jump. As she prepared to leap, she heard Pearl yell. "**Synapseeeeeee.**"

Merrin turned her head and saw Pearl. Pearl looked her way and they grasped hands as they both jumped and sailed to the next neuron.

They landed, with a bit of a bump, on the next neuron's dendrite branch. Both girls were relieved to be together again, and despite having been apart and a little shaken up, they were both intrigued by the nervous system—and they hadn't even made it to the brain yet! Looking forward, they saw something that looked like a sponge—a kind of white, very large sponge. **That has to be the brain**, Pearl thought.

"Merrin, we're about to go into the brain and head to the parietal lobe, where Ms. Anderson will process the hot tea that spilled on her leg. Then we'll go to the frontal lobe to store the memory, so she'll remember how to deal with something like this if it happens again, like getting ice. And then all of this information will be transmitted back to the leg by the motor neuron. Motor neurons are in muscles that will help her move her leg away from the hot tea so more doesn't spill on it. Hold on."

Merrin pointed to all the folds and layers that they gently journeyed up, down, and all around in the brain.

"It looks like tofu even though it's both gray and white," Merrin commented.

And before they knew it, they were headed out of the brain on a motor neuron and down toward Ms. Anderson's leg.

Their nerve impulse took them through the dendrite of the motor neuron and despite the fact that they were again bouncing between one node of Ranvier to the next on the axon part of the neuron, Merrin was still able to notice that their axon had interesting fatty strips on it.

Merrin questioned Pearl, "What's on our axon? I didn't notice these last time. They look like sausages linked together!"

Pearl laughed and nodded in agreement.

"They're fatty myelin sheaths. They protect the axon. See how they are kinda white? That's why the white matter of the brain is called white matter. But I think they look more pinky beige."

Suddenly they heard a **crash**, like something had broken, and then they felt a jolt. The jolt was so abrupt that Pearl dropped to her knees and immediately stopped bouncing along the nodes of Ranvier. She looked up and watched Merrin continue down the neuron.

Ms. Anderson's voice was faint but they could clearly hear her warning the students. "Kids, watch out for the broken tea mug. I need to go get ice for my leg."

Merrin looked back at Pearl who was now up and desperately trying to catch up to her. Merrin turned around and tried to bounce back toward Pearl but the resistance due to the oncoming nerve impulses was too strong. It took all her might to move even an inch. Both girls stretched out their arms and with their fingers barely touching, were able to get close enough to fully grasp each other's hands.

They looked at each other and immediately knew it was time to head out of their Human Body Detectives adventure. They had learned a lot, but it was time to get back. They held on to each other tightly, closed their eyes, and visualized themselves back in Ms. Anderson's classroom. The familiar dizziness started and they felt the twirling and twisting sensation, and then it stopped.

"Merrin, Pearl, are you two OK?" Ms. Anderson asked in a concerned voice. "You're as white as the white matter in your brain. In fact, that's my lesson for today, to discuss white matter—even though it looks more pinky beige," she chuckled, holding a bag of ice to her leg.

"Ahhh, we're fine.

Merrin added, "What happened to your leg?"

Ms. Anderson looked at her strangely as she had thought Merrin was there when it happened. "I clumsily spilled my hot tea on it."

"Ouch, is it OK now?"

"Yes. I reacted and pulled my leg away quite *fast*."

Merrin turned to Pearl and whispered, "Wow, do you think we helped by speeding up her nerve impulses?"

Pearl walked Merrin out of the classroom, and said, "I don't know, but I sure did learn a lot."

"So did I. And our adventure made me hungry," said Merrin. "I'm glad I packed some walnuts in my lunch. Hey, what else did Uncle Nick say we should eat to keep our brains and neurons healthy? They work hard and I can see why they would need lots of good foods."

"Didn't you have a blueberry smoothie and an egg for breakfast? Those both help with brain memory.

"But remember, the brain is made up mostly of water. Drinking water and herbal teas to stay hydrated is really important—it keeps our brains alert. I like how Mom puts lemon slices and mint leaves in our water to flavor it up a bit. And remember those fatty myelin sheaths? They benefit from good fats like avocados, salmon, halibut, and nuts. Some people think the brain looks like a walnut, so they eat walnuts—just like you are—to keep their brains smart!" Pearl added, quite proud of what she already knew.

Merrin said goodbye and Pearl laughed and said, "Have fun in class, Merrin, and use that brain of yours!"

human body detectives®

case solved

CASE FILE #5

How good of a detective
are you?

Can you find
Brainiac?

Let us know how many
times you spotted him at
merrin@drheathernd.com
or pearl@drheathernd.com

More About The Nervous System

Your brain may look like a squishy coiled soft mesh of nothing that is protected by your skull bones, but it is truly the boss of your body; it controls just about everything you do, even when you're snoring away. Your brain is actually works faster than your computer!

There are three major parts of the brain: cerebrum, cerebellum, and the brain stem.

The biggest part of the brain is the **cerebrum**—it's the brains of the brains! The cerebrum looks like a walnut and is located on the outer part of the brain. The cerebrum is not only the thinking part of the brain, it is also responsible for memories, emotions, understanding language, regulating body temperature, eating, and sleeping.

The cerebrum is divided into two equal halves: the right and left hemispheres. The right hemisphere controls the left side of the body and the left hemisphere controls the right side. Nerves through the **corpus collosum** connect these two hemispheres. Each hemisphere has an inside layer called white matter, and an outside layer of gray matter. Research has indicated that the right half helps us think about music, colors, and shapes, and the left half helps us with math, logic, and speech.

The outermost layer of the cerebrum is the **cerebral cortex**. It is divided into four main lobes: frontal, occipital, parietal, and temporal. These lobes have specific functions: **frontal** controls motor functions and memory; **occipital** controls vision and color recognition; **parietal** controls speech and information processing; and **temporal** controls hearing, memory, and emotions.

The **cerebellum** is at the back of the brain below the cerebrum and is about the size of a pear. It may be a lot smaller than the cerebrum, but it has many important jobs, like controlling balance, movement, and coordination. Next time you are riding your bike, give thanks to your cerebellum!

The **brain stem** sits beneath the bottom of the brain just above the neck and connects the brain to the **spinal cord**. Our bodies have voluntary muscles and involuntary muscles. Our voluntary muscles work when we ask them to, like when we want to ride our bikes or move our hand away from a hot stove. Our involuntary muscles, like the heart, lungs, and stomach muscles, are working all the time, automatically. The brain stem is in charge of all the functions of these involuntary muscles to help us circulate our blood, breathe, and digest food. The brain stem is also known as the body's secretary as it sorts through millions of messages that the body and brain send back and forth.

The big questions are: How is the body connected to the brain? And how does the brain know what to tell the body to do? The spinal cord and its nerves put it all together. The **spinal cord** is an extension of the brain. It runs down our backs and is protected by spinal bones (vertebrae). Inside the spinal cord are long bundles of **nerves** that allow messages to be safely communicated between the brain and body.

The brain and the spinal cord make up the **central nervous system (CNS)**, which is the command center, thus leaving the **periphery nervous system (PNS)** consisting of everything outside the CNS. **Neurons** are nerve cells that help transmit information throughout the body. There are three basic parts of a neuron: the **dendrites**, the **cell body**, and the **axon**. Let's say, similar to what happened in the story, you burn yourself, or you are about to burn your hand. Dendrites in your hand will sense heat and will transmit this information down to the cell body and then to the axon. This transmission will continue from neuron to neuron—via **synapses**—until it reaches the brain. The brain will then send a message through neurons to your muscles telling you to take your hand away from the heat. This action may happen at a speed of up to 200 miles per hour!

There is a lot more to learn about the brain, and scientists are working every day to learn more about this complex organ. Maybe you can grow up and be a scientist who studies the brain! In the meantime, take good care of your brain by protecting it by wearing helmets when on a bike, scooter, or skateboard, and feed it healthy foods like fish, nuts, and seeds!

Your Brain

The Human Body Detectives discovered these different parts of the brain.

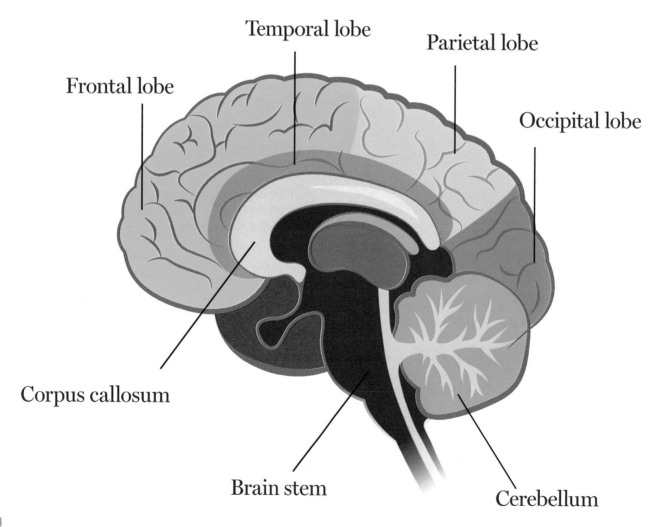

Temporal lobe

Parietal lobe

Frontal lobe

Occipital lobe

Corpus callosum

Brain stem

Cerebellum

Your Neuron

The neuron is pretty interesting, it is made up of several parts.

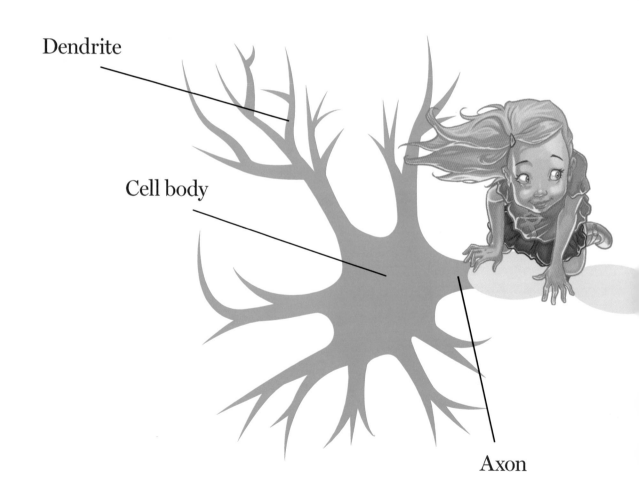

Dendrite

Cell body

Axon

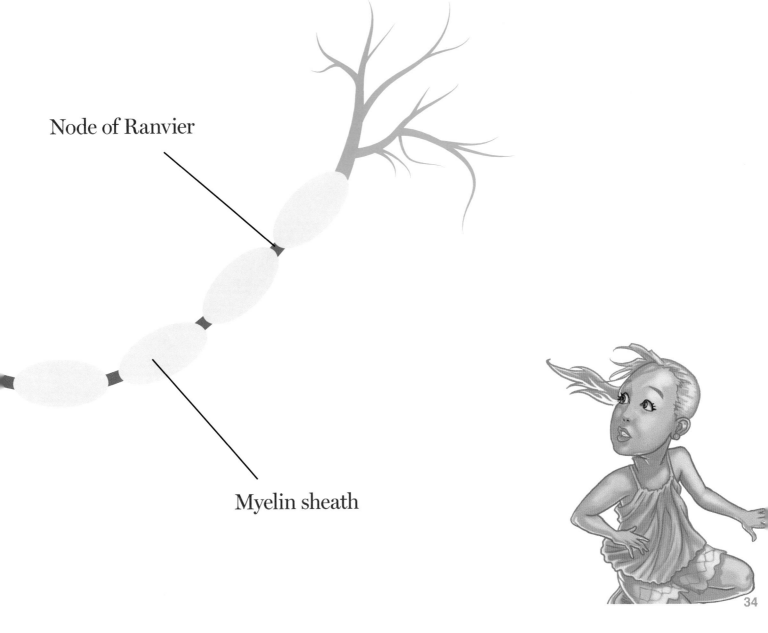

Node of Ranvier

Myelin sheath

Human Body Detectives Ask You...

Both Merrin and Pearl are fascinated by the brain. They learned some interesting and intriguing facts that they wanted to share with you.

did you know that...

* the brain is always working, even while you sleep?

* more than 90% of the world is right-handed?

* your brain is about 2% of your total body?

* there are about 100 billion neurons in the human brain, the same number of stars in our galaxy?

* the average human dream lasts only 2 to 3 seconds?

* your brain can go without oxygen for 3 to 5 minutes before injury will occur?

* your brain consumes as much as a fifth of all the energy you get from food?

* the word "dendrite" (the part of a neuron that brings information toward the cell body) comes from the Greek word meaning "tree"?

* information travels in the nerves at speeds of more than 200 miles per hour or 429 kilometers/hour?

* a jellyfish doesn't have a brain?

* the average human brain weighs about 3 pounds (1.4 kilograms)?

* the part of the brain called the "amygdala" gets its name from the Greek word for "almond" because the shapes are similar?

* the length of myelinated fatty nerve fibers in the brain is 241,000 to 289,000 miles or 150,000 to180,000 km?

* sixty percent of an octopus's nerve cells are located in its arms?

* a doctor who studies nerves is called a neurologist?

* the Swahili word for brain is "ubongo"?

* though the brain may process pain messages, it doesn't feel pain.

Brain Metaphors

Merrin and Pearl love to use their brains. One of the ways they do that is through metaphors, which compares two things that seem unlikely to be similar.

The following lists some of the things that the brain has been compared to and describes why they are similar the brain.

The brain is . . .

- A spider web because it is delicate and connects to many things.

- A tree because it has branches that go this way and that way.

- A symphony because it creates movement, ideas, and emotions.

Can you think of more?

Human Body Detectives
and Brain Health

Brain power.

Fuel your brain by drinking lots of water and eating healthy foods like eggs, blueberries, wild salmon, avocados, nuts, seeds, and bananas.

Brain protection.

Always wear a helmet when you're doing things like riding a bike, skateboard, or scooter, so you're safe if you fall off and your brain won't get hurt.

Brain workout.

Challenge your brain with activities such as puzzles, reading, playing music, making art, or anything else that gets your brain thinking a little more.

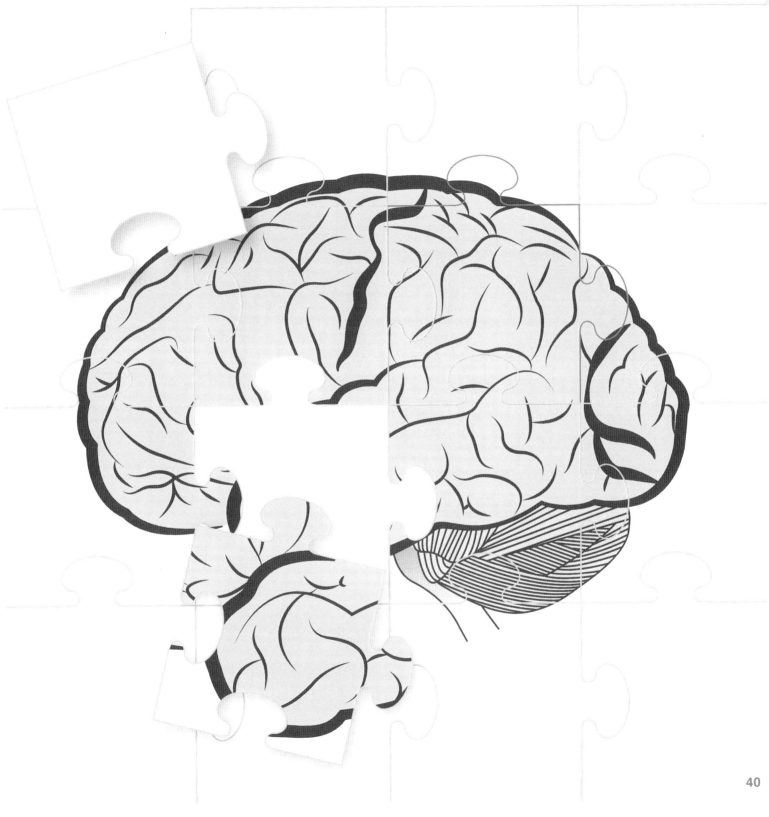

Brain Teasers and More

We all love a good joke and the Human Body Detectives have found a few that will make you laugh out loud!

What did the right hemisphere say to the left hemisphere when they could not agree on anything?

Let's split.

What street does the hippocampus live on?

Memory Lane.

What did parietal say to frontal?

I lobe you.

When does a brain get afraid?

When it loses its nerves.

Why was the neuron sent to the principal's office?

It had trouble controlling its impulses.

What do you get when you cross a thought with a light bulb?

A bright idea.

What does a brain do when it sees a friend across the street?

Gives her a brain wave.

What works even after it is fired?

A neuron.

Glossary

A list of useful brain words and their meaning.

Axon (ak-son): Part of the neuron that transmits impulses.

Brain matter (breyn mat-er) There is white and gray matter in the brain that make up the brain matter. The white matter is mostly made up of axons, whereas the grey matter contains the cell bodies and dendrites.

Brain stem (breyn stem) The brain stem connects the brain to the spinal cord and controls the muscles in your body that work automatically, all the time: muscles that help with breathing, digesting food, and circulating blood.

Cell body (sel bod-ee) The cell body is the body of neuron.

Central nervous system (CNS) (sen-trul nur-vuh s-sis-tuh m) The CNS is part of the nervous system consisting of the brain and spinal cord.

Cerebrum (suh-REE-brum) The cerebrum is the biggest part of the brain and it controls the voluntary muscles that you choose to use (like when you use your leg muscles to kick a soccer ball).

Cerebellum (sair-uh-BELL-um) The cerebellum is at the back of the brain and controls balance, movement, and coordination.

Dendrite (den-drahyt) Dendrites arc the branching parts that extend from the axon and aid in the transmission of nerve impulses.

Myelin sheath (my-e-lin sheth) Myelin sheaths wrap around axons to protect and speed up nerve impulses.

Nerve (nurv) A nerve conducts impulses between the brain or spinal cord and the other parts of the body.

Neuron (noo-ron) A neuron is a bundle of nerves that has a cell body, dendrites, and an axon.

Node of Ranvier (nohd-ov-Ran·vier) Nodes of Ranvier are gaps located on the myelin sheaths of the axon that help with the transmission of nerve impulses.

Periphery nervous system (PNS) (puh-rif-uh-ree-nur-vuh s-sis-tuh m) The PNS consists of nerves outside the spinal cord and brain.

Synapse (sin-aps) A synapse occurs between dendrites and helps nerve impulses pass from one neuron to another.

Dr. Heather Manley, ND, is a practicing physician who received her medical degree in 2001 from National College of Naturopathic Medicine in Portland, Oregon. She is also the award-winning author of the **Human Body Detectives** book and curriculum series.

A contributing writer to Dandelion Moms, Organic Eats magazine, Parents Canada, and KIWI magazine, Dr. Heather was inspired to write the **Human Body Detectives** stories when she went on a search for books about healthy eating tips for parents and kids and couldn't find what she was looking for. She wanted to provide a fun and engaging resource that would teach kids about how their bodies work and what foods best feed them. And the HBDs were born.

The **Human Body Detectives** series won Moms' Choice Award and is also a Parent Tested, Parent Approved winner. Dr. Heather has been named to the Top 50 Mompreneurs Bloggers List on both **Babble**, **VoiceBoks** and **blogtrepreneur**.

Dr. Heather lives and practices on the Big Island of Hawaii, where her focus is on preventative healthcare for families and providing a resource for families to learn more about preventative health care so that they can be confident and proactive in their everyday health. She lives with her husband and her two daughters, with whom she based her stories' characters, Merrin and Pearl.

www.humanbodydetectives.com

Visit **humanbodydetectives.com** to join the HBD mailing list and receive a free HBD and proactive health guide.

 visit us on Facebook: HumanBodyDetectives

 tweet with Dr. Heather on Twitter: drheathernd

I AM GRATEFUL

Each time I sit down to write my next Human Body Detectives book and curriculum, I am unsure about which physiological system I will have Merrin and Pearl journey into. I am completely fascinated by the human body and how it works diligently to keep us alive and healthy. I strive to find the foundation of each system to help kids (and their parents and teachers) completely grasp how it works and what foods will best fuel it.

I am always very appreciative for my family, friends, colleagues, and all of my customers who are constantly supporting me. Thank you so much!

I also need to bow my head to Nina Jones (jonesy.ca), who has been with me from the beginning, adding her magic touch in layout and formatting; Jessica Swift, of Swift Ink Editorial Services, for her genius editing; and SF300 for creating the exact images I have wanted for each book.

I could not ask for a better group of people to work with.

Now, on to the next HBD book! Stay tuned!

Dr. Heal

FURTHER SPECIAL THANKS

When deciding to write about the brain and nervous system, the company Nordic Naturals helped inspire me. Their devotion to educating the public on the topic of omega-3 deficiency in children—which is critical in the healthy development of the brain—plus their outstanding children's line of omega-3 fish oil and multivitamins, led me to write Brainiacs as a way to further educate children about how their brains work and why feeding it well is so very important. Thank you, Nordic Naturals, for the valuable, educational, and inspirational work that you do.

43807274R00031

Made in the USA
Lexington, KY
13 August 2015